W9-BRI-715

DINOSAURS

SMALL & DEADLY DINOSAURS

Brenda Ralph Lewis

GARETH**STEVENS**
GS
PUBLISHING
A Member of the WRC Media Family of Companies

Please visit our Web site at: **www.garethstevens.com**
For a free color catalog describing Gareth Stevens Publishing's
list of high-quality books and multimedia programs,
call 1-800-542-2595 (USA) or 1-800-387-3178 (Canada).
Gareth Stevens Publishing's fax: (414) 332-3567.

Library of Congress Cataloging-in-Publication Data

Lewis, Brenda Ralph.
    Small & deadly dinosaurs / Brenda Ralph Lewis.
      p. cm. — (Nature's monsters. Dinosaurs)
    Includes bibliographical references and index.
    ISBN-10: 0-8368-6846-3 — ISBN-13: 978-0-8368-6846-3 (lib. bdg.)
    1. Dinosaurs—Juvenile literature. 2. Predatory animals—Juvenile literature.
 I. Small and deadly dinosaurs. II. Title. III. Series.
 QE861.5.L496   2006
 567.9—dc22   2006042357

This North American edition first published in 2007 by
Gareth Stevens Publishing
A Member of the WRC Media Family of Companies
330 West Olive Street, Suite 100
Milwaukee, WI 53212 USA

Original edition and illustrations copyright © 2006 by International Masters Publishers AB.
Produced by Amber Books Ltd., Bradley's Close, 74–77 White Lion Street, London N1 9PF, U.K.

Project editor: Michael Spilling
Design: Graham Curd

Gareth Stevens editorial direction: Valerie J. Weber
Gareth Stevens editor: Leifa Butrick
Gareth Stevens art direction: Tammy West
Gareth Stevens production: Jessica Morris

Printed in the United States of America

1 2 3 4 5 6 7 8 9 10 09 08 07 06

Contents

Continents of the World

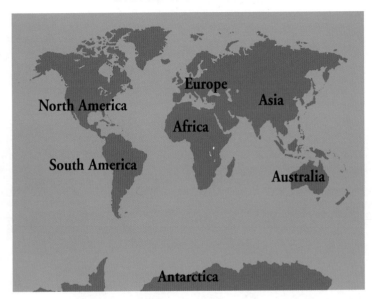

The world is divided into seven continents — North America, South America, Europe, Africa, Asia, Australia, and Antarctica. On the following pages, the area where each dinosaur was discovered is shown in red, while all land is shown in green.

Words that appear in the glossary are printed in **boldface** type the first time they occur in the text.

Coelophysis

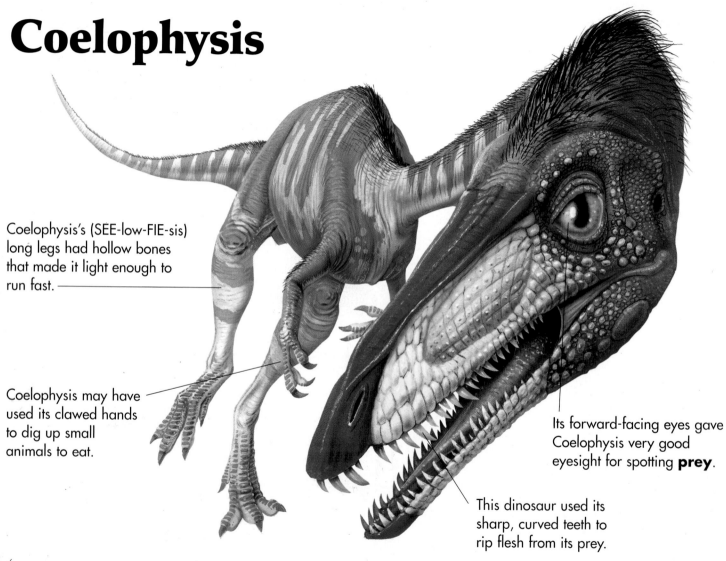

Coelophysis's (SEE-low-FIE-sis) long legs had hollow bones that made it light enough to run fast.

Coelophysis may have used its clawed hands to dig up small animals to eat.

Its forward-facing eyes gave Coelophysis very good eyesight for spotting **prey**.

This dinosaur used its sharp, curved teeth to rip flesh from its prey.

Coelophysis was an **omnivore**. It would eat anything. **Paleontologists** have found the bones of fish and small reptiles in the stomachs of Coelophysis. Coelophysis was also a **cannibal**.

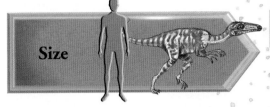

Size

1 Sometimes, Coelophysis had to search hard for food. This Coelophysis family is lucky. They discover a **carcass** and feed hungrily on its flesh. They do not know that three other hungry Coelophysis are hiding nearby.

The three Coelophysis have not been able to find other prey, except for **dinosaurs** of their own kind. They jump out from behind the ferns, grab some of the young Coelophysis in their big mouths, **2** and run off into the forest.

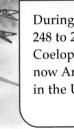

Where in the World

During the **Triassic** period, 248 to 206 million years ago, Coelophysis lived in what is now Arizona and New Mexico in the United States.

Compsognathus

Compsognathus's thick coat of **bristles** may have kept it warm at night.

For such a tiny dinosaur, Compsognathus had powerful legs and feet.

Compsognathus (KOMP-sog-NAH-thus) had huge eyes that helped it see clearly at night.

Compsognathus held its prey tightly with its strong hands and long claws.

Although Compsognathus was the smallest dinosaur of them all, it was an extremely fast runner. Small lizards and animals would have to move very quickly to avoid being eaten by Compsognathus.

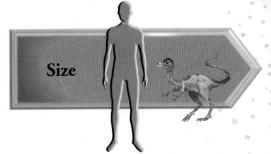

Compsognathus was the smallest of all dinosaurs. It was about 3 feet (1 meter) long and weighed less than 8 pounds (3.5 kilograms) — not much more than a large chicken or small turkey.

1 Compsognathus lived on insects and small lizards. It searched for its food on land and in rivers and lakes.

2 Lizards can move fast, but Compsognathus was faster. A Compsognathus uses its strong hind legs and easily catches up with a lizard. It seizes the lizard in its sharp teeth, then crushes it and eats it.

Where in the World

Compsognathus lived during the **Jurassic** period, from 206 to 144 million years ago. Fossils have been found in two places in Europe — Cajuer in southern France and Solnhofen in Bavaria, southern Germany.

Deinonychus

Deinonychus (die-NON-nih-kus) was able to move its short but **flexible** neck very quickly.

Open spaces in Deinonychus's skull made its large head light.

Deinonychus bit its prey so forcefully that many of its teeth broke.

The huge claw that grew on each hind foot gave Deinonychus its name. *Deinonychus* means "terrible claw."

Deinonychus measured less than 11 feet (3.4 m) long and 6 feet (1.8 m) tall. It was small, but its teeth and claws were terrible weapons against much larger dinosaurs.

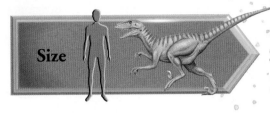

In the movie *Jurassic Park* (1993), Deinonychus was the model for all the **predators** who appeared in the film. In real life, Deinonychus lived 100 million years after Jurassic times.

1 The plant-eating Iguanodon is almost three times the size of Deinonychus, but it cannot escape when four of the small dinosaurs attack at the same time.

2 The Iguanodon roars with pain and falls over. It weighs 4.5 tons (4 metric tons) and kills one Deinonychus by falling on it.

3 While the attackers feast on the Iguanodon's flesh, four more Deinonychus try to join in. The first three use their teeth and claws against the newcomers in a fierce fight to keep their prey for themselves.

During the **Cretaceous** period, from 144 to 65 million years ago, Deinonychus lived in what is now Wyoming, Oklahoma, Montana, Utah, and Maryland.

Edmontonia

Edmontonia (ed-mon-TONE-ee-ah) had armor all over — even to the tip of its tail, which was **studded** with **spikes**.

Thick **slabs** of bone protected Edmontonia's flat head.

The dinosaur had a few leaf-shaped teeth at the back of its mouth.

Edmontonia weighed up to 3 tons (2.7 metric tons) and had strong legs like **pillars**.

Because of its thick body armor, some people have compared Edmontonia to an army tank used in modern warfare. Edmontonia needed its armor for protection against meat-eating dinosaurs.

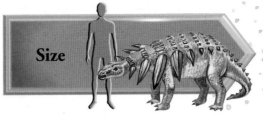

Size

1   Edmontonia is too heavy to move fast. Running away will not save it from attack. When an Albertosaurus — a meat-eating dinosaur — approaches, this Edmontonia does not try to escape.

2   The Albertosaurus thinks it is going to get an easy meal. It runs toward the Edmontonia, its jaws open, ready to take a big bite. Suddenly, the Edmontonia gets up. One of the long, sharp spikes along its sides stabs the Albertosaurus in the neck and kills it.

Where in the World

Scientists found Edmontonia fossils in the Edmonton Rock Formation near the Red Deer River in Alberta, Canada. The dinosaur lived there during the Cretaceous period, from 144 to 65 million years ago.

Gallimimus

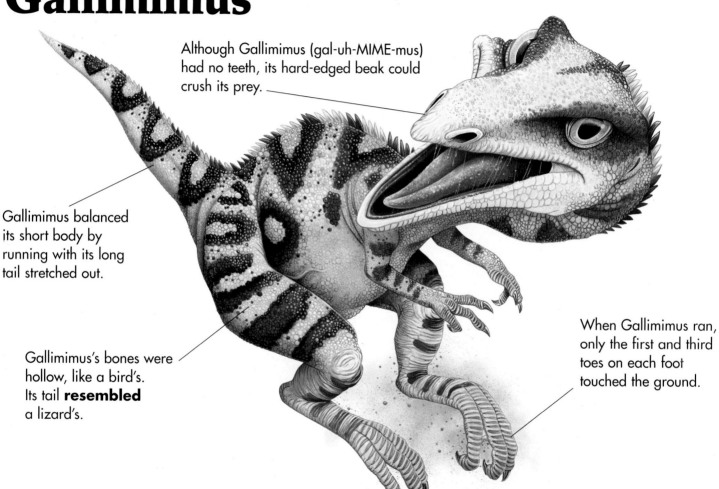

Although Gallimimus (gal-uh-MIME-mus) had no teeth, its hard-edged beak could crush its prey.

Gallimimus balanced its short body by running with its long tail stretched out.

Gallimimus's bones were hollow, like a bird's. Its tail **resembled** a lizard's.

When Gallimimus ran, only the first and third toes on each foot touched the ground.

Gallimimus was both a plant eater and a meat eater. It lived on **foliage** but also ate insects and small animals, such as lizards. The Gallimimus liked eggs, too.

Size

Gallimimus had long, **slender** legs like an ostrich and could probably move as fast. Ostriches can run up to 43 miles (70 kilometers) per hour.

1 A Gallimimus discovers a nest full of eggs belonging to another dinosaur. The nest is buried in the ground, but the Gallimimus soon digs it up with its long, clawed fingers.

2 Quickly, the Gallimimus cracks the shells of all but one of the eggs and swallows the contents. Suddenly, it sees another Gallimimus moving toward the nest.

3 The newcomer is large and fierce. The Gallimimus decides not to fight it. It grabs the last egg in its beak and runs away.

Where in the World

A team of Russian paleontologists first discovered Gallimimus fossils in 1972 in southeastern Mongolia. The half-bird, half-lizard dinosaur lived during the Cretaceous period, from 144 to 65 million years ago.

Herrerasaurus

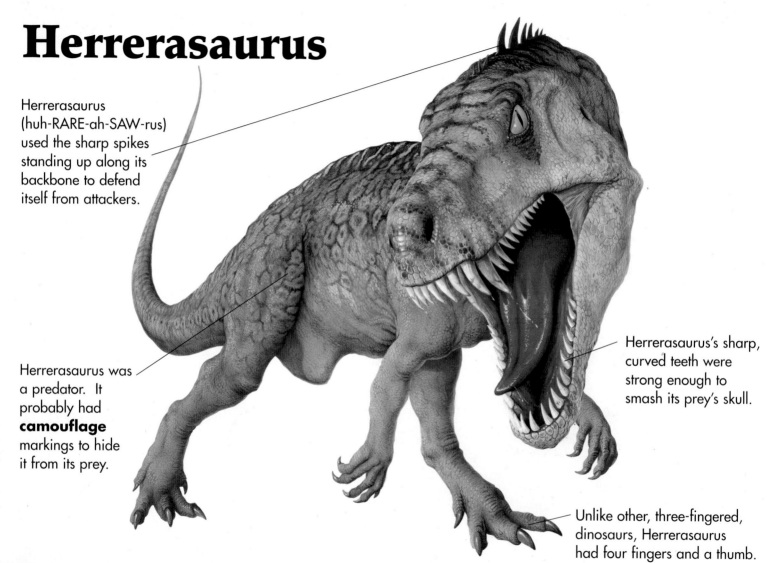

Herrerasaurus (huh-RARE-ah-SAW-rus) used the sharp spikes standing up along its backbone to defend itself from attackers.

Herrerasaurus was a predator. It probably had **camouflage** markings to hide it from its prey.

Herrerasaurus's sharp, curved teeth were strong enough to smash its prey's skull.

Unlike other, three-fingered, dinosaurs, Herrerasaurus had four fingers and a thumb.

Today, wolves bite each other's heads when they fight. Herrerasaurus did the same millions of years ago. Paleontologists have found teeth marks on the **fossilized** skulls of Herrerasaurus.

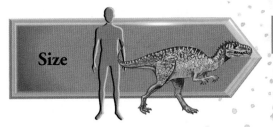

Size

1 A young Herrerasaurus discovers a large carcass and starts ripping away at the flesh. Before long, another, older, Herrerasaurus arrives on the scene. It wants the carcass for itself. The older Herrerasaurus opens it jaws very wide and bites the younger one hard.

2 The older Herrerasaurus holds the younger one's head in an unbreakable grip as its teeth slice into the skull. The younger one screams with pain. It has to wait until its attacker lets go before it can run away and hide.

Did You Know?

Herrerasaurus was one of the earliest dinosaurs to live on Earth. Like all meat-eating dinosaurs, Herrerasaurus was a **theropod** — it walked and ran on its two powerful back legs.

Where in the World

The first Herrerasaurus fossil was found in 1958 by Victorino Herrera on his ranch in Argentina, South America. Herrerasaurus lived in Argentina during the Triassic period, from 248 to 206 million years ago.

15

Hypsilophodon

Hypsilophodon (hip-seh-LOFF-oh-don) had long shins and short muscular thighs good for running fast over short distances.

The dinosaur's skull was quite small — only as long as a human hand.

Hypsilophodon used its teeth for grinding. It was one of the few dinosaurs able to chew its food.

Hypsilophodon was unusual among plant-eating dinosaurs, which were mostly huge and slow. Hypsilophodon was only 6.5 feet (2 m) long and could run fast.

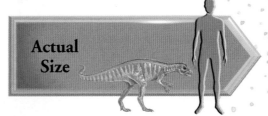

Actual Size

1 A Hypsilophodon herd with several young Hypsilophodon is grazing in a forest. Suddenly, a huge meat eater, a Baryonyx, leaps out from behind the trees. Very frightened, the Hypsilophodon flee in all directions.

2 The Baryonyx thought it might be easy to catch and eat the young Hypsilophodon. The Baryonyx was wrong. The Hypsilophodon run away so fast that the huge and heavy Baryonyx cannot catch them.

Where in the World

Hypsilophodon fossils have been found in southern England, Spain, and South Dakota, where they lived during the Cretaceous period, from 144 to 65 million years ago.

Ornitholestes

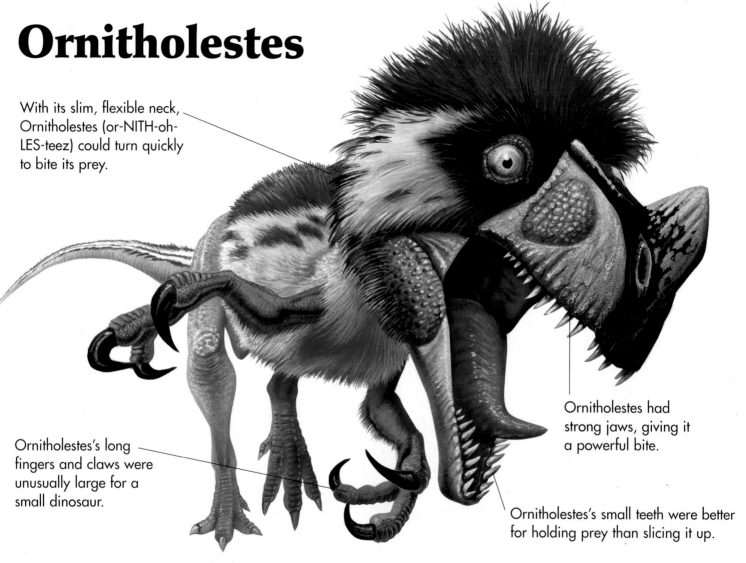

With its slim, flexible neck, Ornitholestes (or-NITH-oh-LES-teez) could turn quickly to bite its prey.

Ornitholestes had strong jaws, giving it a powerful bite.

Ornitholestes's long fingers and claws were unusually large for a small dinosaur.

Ornitholestes's small teeth were better for holding prey than slicing it up.

In **prehistoric** times, bad weather made life difficult for Ornitholestes and other dinosaurs. Extreme cold or heat, as well as too much rain or not enough, could make it hard to find food.

1 There has been no rain for a long time, and a **drought** has followed. The parents of three baby Ornitholestes have to hunt over long distances for food. They find a lizard and feed it to their young, but they cannot find any more food.

Size

Without enough food, the baby Ornitholestes grow weaker and weaker. Eventually, they die from starvation. Their parents are starving, too. The only food **2** they have is their dead babies, so they eat them.

Where in the World

Ornitholestes lived during the Jurassic period, from 206 to 144 million years ago. Fossils have been found in Utah and Wyoming, close to the the eastern side of the Rocky Mountains.

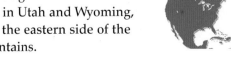

Oviraptor

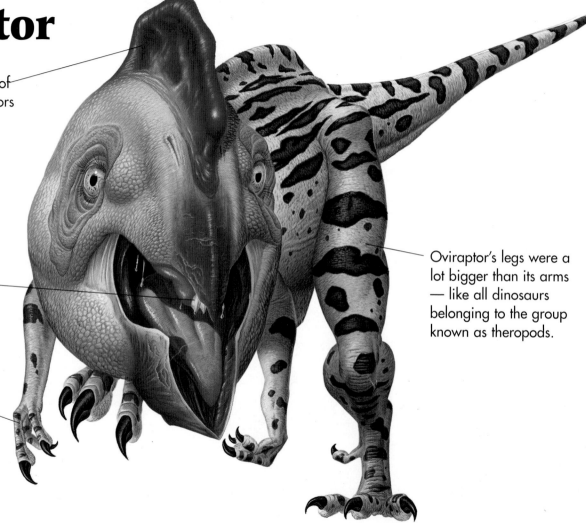

The **crests** on the heads of male and female Oviraptors (OH-vih-RAP-tors) were different.

Oviraptor had two teeth shaped like pegs in the top of its beak.

Oviraptor's large hands could fold up like the wings of a bird.

Oviraptor's legs were a lot bigger than its arms — like all dinosaurs belonging to the group known as theropods.

Paleontologists once believed that Oviraptors stole eggs from other dinosaurs. Then, a fossilized Oviraptor was found on a nest of its own eggs. Oviraptor was not a thief after all.

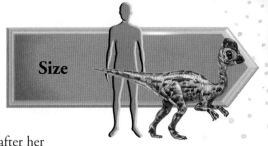

Size

1 A mother Oviraptor looks after her nest full of eggs. From time to time, she turns them gently, just as birds do today.

2 As she sits on the nest, the mother's body heat keeps the eggs warm. Suddenly, a strong wind starts to blow, but she stays on the nest, protecting her eggs.

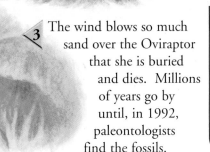

3 The wind blows so much sand over the Oviraptor that she is buried and dies. Millions of years go by until, in 1992, paleontologists find the fossils.

Where in the World

The first Oviraptor fossil was found in 1924 in Mongolia. Since then, more skeletons have been found in Mongolia, where it lived during the Cretaceous period, from 144 to 65 million years ago.

Protoceratops

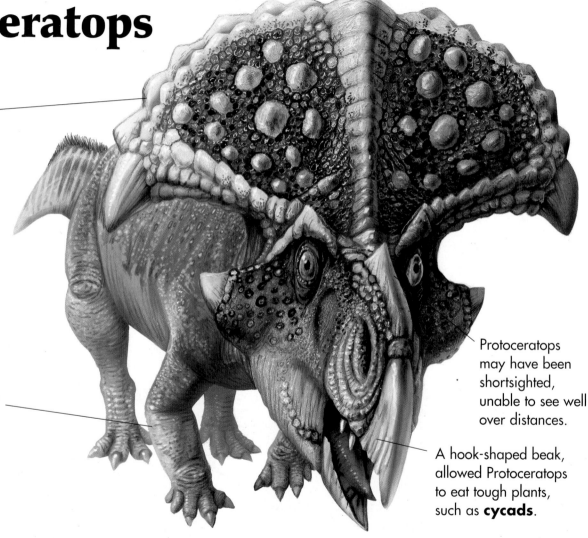

Protoceratops's (PRO-toh-SER-ah-tops) big neck frill was held up by bone **struts**, not plates.

With front legs shorter than its hind legs, Protoceratops leaned forward to walk.

Protoceratops may have been shortsighted, unable to see well over distances.

A hook-shaped beak, allowed Protoceratops to eat tough plants, such as **cycads**.

Protoceratops was a plant eater, and like many plant-eating dinosaurs, it lived in herds. They stayed together for protection from attack by meat eaters and to keep their young safe.

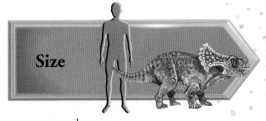

Size

1 The two Velociraptors approaching a herd of Protoceratops are very hungry. They think that one of the two babies in the herd would make a good meal. The big adult Protoceratops close around the babies to guard them against attack.

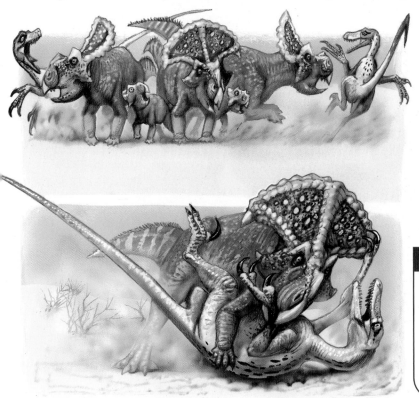

The Velociraptors keep trying to get the babies. Then, one of them gets too close. An adult Protoceratops gets angry and attacks. Using its strong, sharp claws, it rips the Velociraptor's flesh and crushes its bones. **2**

Where in the World

Protoceratops lived in North America and in Mongolia, eastern Asia, during the Cretaceous period, from 144 to 65 million years ago. Asia and North America were one land mass then.

Psittacosaurus

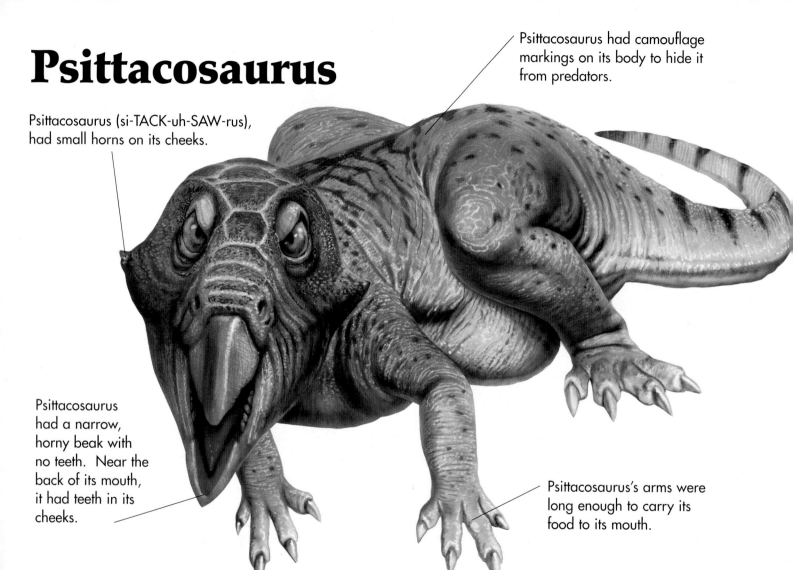

Psittacosaurus (si-TACK-uh-SAW-rus), had small horns on its cheeks.

Psittacosaurus had camouflage markings on its body to hide it from predators.

Psittacosaurus had a narrow, horny beak with no teeth. Near the back of its mouth, it had teeth in its cheeks.

Psittacosaurus's arms were long enough to carry its food to its mouth.

A plant eater, Psittacosaurus had strong arms and hands for holding down branches. Its beak was lined with razor-sharp horns, which it used to strip leaves off branches.

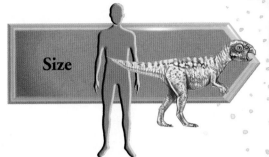

Size

Did You Know?

Every year, each Psittacosaurus added another line to the growth lines on its bones. Paleontologists who have counted these lines think that Psittacosaurus could have lived to be eleven years old.

1 Three Psittacosaurus are feasting in the forest. They can easily reach plenty of low branches. While one Psittacosaurus stuffs itself full of leaves, another cracks cones in its mouth to get at the juicy seeds inside.

2 One Psittacosaurus eats too much. It is too full and feels uncomfortable. To **digest** the food, the Psittacosaurus swallows some pebbles, which **grind** up the food in its stomach.

Where in the World

Psittacosaurus lived during the early Cretaceous period, from 144 to 127 million years ago. They make up 90 percent of all dinosaur fossils found in Mongolia. Other Psittacosaurus fossils were found in Thailand, China, and Russia.

Troödon

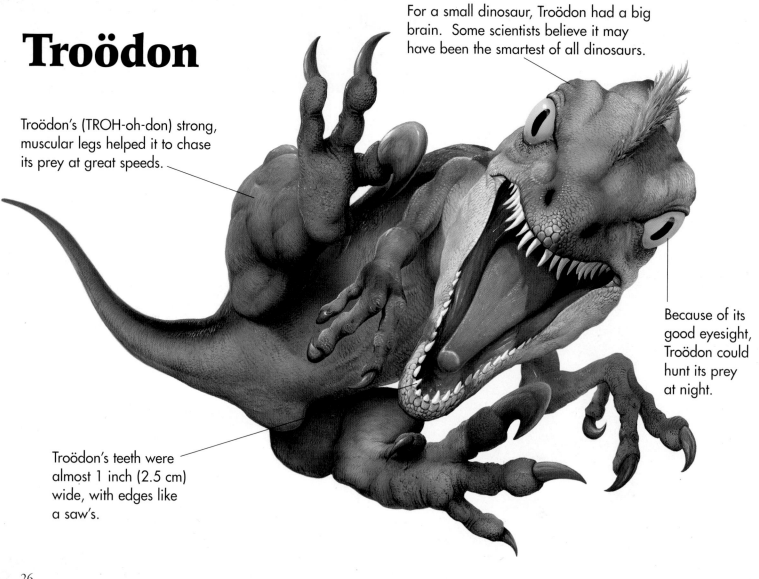

For a small dinosaur, Troödon had a big brain. Some scientists believe it may have been the smartest of all dinosaurs.

Troödon's (TROH-oh-don) strong, muscular legs helped it to chase its prey at great speeds.

Because of its good eyesight, Troödon could hunt its prey at night.

Troödon's teeth were almost 1 inch (2.5 cm) wide, with edges like a saw's.

Troödon mothers laid up to twenty-two eggs, in pairs, all at the same time. Many Troödon eggs found by paleontologists still had the **original** shells around them.

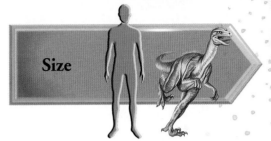

Size

1 After laying their eggs, Troödon mothers arranged them very carefully. The eggs were partly buried in soil to keep them from moving. If the eggs moved before the babies hatched, the young Troödons might die, or be born with **deformities**.

2 Like many birds today, Troödon parents took turns sitting on the eggs and keeping them warm until they hatched. Baby Troödons came out of their eggs perfectly formed, tiny copies of their parents.

Where in the World

During the Cretaceous period from 144 to 65 million years ago, Troödon lived in Montana, Wyoming, and Alberta, Canada. The first fossils were found in 1855.

Velociraptor

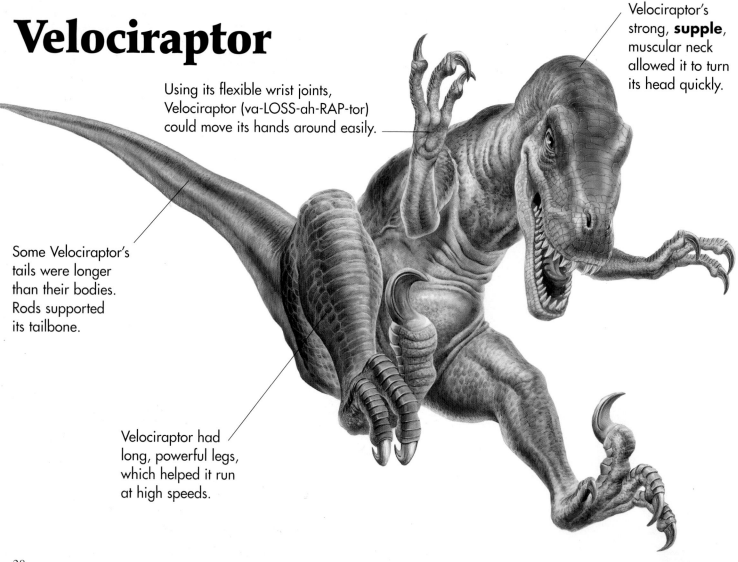

Velociraptor's strong, **supple**, muscular neck allowed it to turn its head quickly.

Using its flexible wrist joints, Velociraptor (va-LOSS-ah-RAP-tor) could move its hands around easily.

Some Velociraptor's tails were longer than their bodies. Rods supported its tailbone.

Velociraptor had long, powerful legs, which helped it run at high speeds.

Velociraptor was a small dinosaur. Velociraptors may have formed gangs to hunt prey bigger than themselves. When hunting smaller prey, a single Velociraptor could do the job on its own.

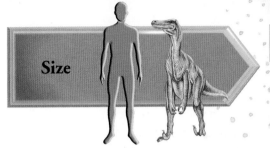

Size

Did You Know?

In 2005, British scientists, using a special robot leg, discovered that Velociraptor used its leg claw to hold down its prey. Earlier, they thought that Velociraptor sliced flesh with it.

1 Velociraptor was one of the smarter dinosaurs. When hunting, it watched a herd of dinosaurs for a while, looking for a young, old, or sick animal that could be caught easily. When Velociraptor found what it wanted, it attacked with its claws and teeth.

2 Two Velociraptors attack a group of Gallimimus. The Gallimimus cannot defend themselves and one is soon dying on the ground. It is still alive, however, when the Velociraptor starts to eat its flesh. The Velociraptor tears out big chunks and swallows them whole.

Where in the World

Velociraptor lived in Mongolia and parts of China during the Cretaceous period, from 144 to 65 million years ago. The first Velociraptor fossils were found at Flaming Cliffs, Mongolia, in 1923.

Glossary

ancestors — people or animals in a family or group who lived in earlier times

bristles — short, stiff, rough hairs

camouflage — the pattern on an animal's skin that helps it hide in its environment

cannibal — an animal that eats other creatures of its own kind

carcass — the dead body of an animal, especially one that has been killed for food

crests — raised lines or ridges of skin on an animal

Cretaceous — a period of time from 144 to 65 million years ago, when dinosaurs roamed Earth

cycads — fern-like trees that grow seed cones and are found in warm areas of Earth

deformities — where something's original shape has been changed and often damaged

digest — to break down food in the gut so it can be used by the body for energy and strength

dinosaurs — various reptiles that lived on Earth from 245 to 65 million years ago but have since died out

drought — a long period when rain does not fall, causing the soil to dry up and plant life to die

flexible — able to bend easily without breaking

foliage — the leaves that grow on the branches of trees or on the stems of plants

fossils — remains or imprints of animals and dinosaurs from an earlier time, often prehistoric; fossils are found beneath Earth's surface, pressed into rocks

fossilized — referring to something that has become a fossil

grind — to crush or reduce to powder

Jurassic — a period of time from 206 to 144 million years ago, when birds first appeared

omnivore — an animal that can eat both meat and plants

original — from the very beginning, the first of its kind

paleontologists — scientists who study plant and animal life in prehistoric times (before human life began on Earth)

pillars — upright columns used as supports for something

predators — animals that hunt other animals for food

prehistoric — the time before human history began

prey — an animal hunted for food

resembled — looked like or was almost the same as

slabs — broad, flat pieces

slender — thin or narrow

spikes — sharp, pointed objects sticking out or upward

squawk — a harsh, sudden scream

struts — lengths of bone, wood, metal, or other strong material used to support and strengthen

studded — covered with studs or spikes

supple — able to bend or twist easily without breaking

theropod — a meat-eating dinosaur that walked on two legs

Triassic — a period of time from 248 to 206 million years ago, when many reptiles, including dinosaurs, first appeared

For More Information

Books

Dinosaurs!: The Biggest, Baddest, Strangest, Fastest.
   Howard Zimmerman (Atheneum)

*Dougal Dixon's Amazing Dinosaurs: The Fiercest,
   the Tallest, the Toughest, the Smallest.*
   Dougal Dixon (Boyds Mills Press)

Nest of Dinosaurs: The Story of the Oviraptor.
   Mark Norell and Lowell Dingus
   (Doubleday Books for Young Readers)

Small and Scary. Discovering Dinosaurs (series).
   Michael Benton (Chrysalis Books)

Velociraptor and Other Small, Speedy, Meat-Eaters.
   Virginia Schomp (Benchmark Books)

Web Sites

Dinosaur Illustrations
www.search4dinosaurs.com

Dinosaurs Online
www.kidsturncentral.com/links/dinolinks.htm

Dinosaur Timeline
www.kidport.com/RefLib/Science/Dinosaurs/
   DinoTimeline.htm

Dinosaur Time Machine
www.mantyweb.com/dinosaur

Kokoro Dinosaurs
www.kokorodinosaurs.com/index.html

Publisher's note to educators and parents: Our editors have
carefully reviewed these Web sites to ensure that they are suitable for
children. Many Web sites change frequently, however, and we cannot
guarantee that a site's future contents will continue to meet our high
standards of quality and educational value. Be advised that children
should be closely supervised whenever they access the Internet.

Index